MUSIC THROUGH TIME

Pauline Hall & Paul Harris

Piano Book 2

CONTENTS

MUSIC DEPARTMENT

OXFORD
UNIVERSITY PRESS

1625
A Toye

Giles Farnaby
(1563–1640)

Charles I became King of England and married Henrietta Maria, a French princess. Due to an outbreak of the plague in London, Parliament met in Oxford. The first fire engine—horse drawn, of course— appeared in England.

Giles Farnaby was an English composer who is particularly known for writing madrigals (pieces for unaccompanied choir). The 'Toye' was a name given to short pieces of this time, usually written for the lute.

This is the year in which the Italian composer Domenico Mazzochi is said to have been the first composer to use < and > to indicate crescendo and diminuendo.

Anne Cromwell was a cousin of Oliver Cromwell, and a keen amateur player. She made this collection of short pieces to play for the entertainment of her family and friends. Many pieces were arrangements of popular tunes of the day.

1638

A Masque

Anne Cromwell's Virginal Book

(17th century)

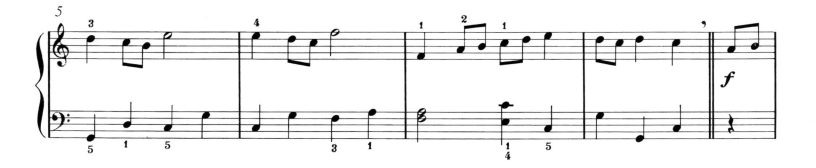

1695
Hornpipe

Henry Purcell
(1659–95)

In England, a tax on windows was introduced, eventually being charged on every house with more than six. It remained in force until 1851, and many people bricked up their extra windows to avoid paying.

The hornpipe is a dance traditionally associated with sailors. This particular one is arranged from some incidental music Purcell wrote for the play *The Moor's Revenge*.

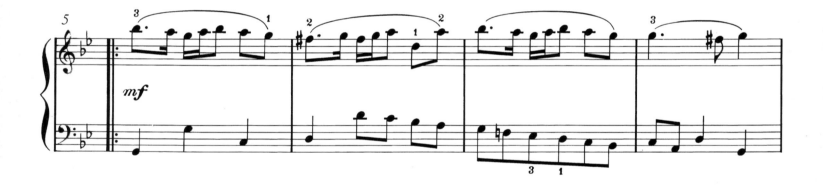

This was the time that bloodthirsty pirates sailed the high seas.
They lived mostly on the islands of Hispaniola and Jamaica,
and struck fear into the hearts of ordinary sea-voyagers.

Jeremiah Clarke is probably best remembered for his *Prince of
Denmark's March* (better known as the *Trumpet Voluntary*).
He was organist at St Paul's Cathedral for many years.

1700
King William's March

Jeremiah Clarke
(*c.*1670–1707)

Silent Worship

George Frideric Handel
(1685–1759)

Vivaldi wrote his famous violin concertos, *The Four Seasons*. Vitus Bering discovered the channel between Siberia and Alaska—now called the Bering Straits.

Handel's father opposed the idea of a career in music for his son, who studied law instead until his father's death. This tune was originally a trio for two violins and keyboard and then later used as a song—Handel often re-used the same music for different pieces.

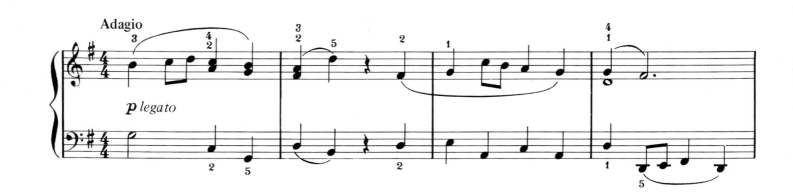

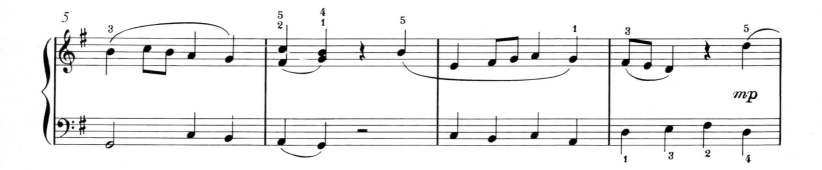

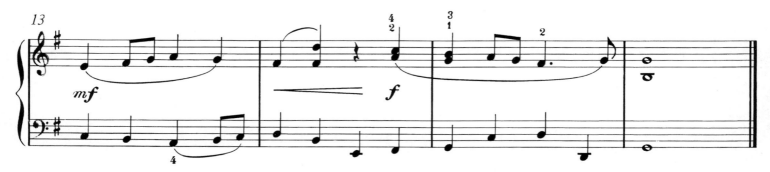

With the growth of science and the decline of belief in magic, superstitious British laws against witchcraft were finally repealed. India Rubber (the type found at the top of your pencils) first appeared in Britain.

John Sheeles lived in England during the first half of the 18th century, and was a noted composer and harpsichord player.

1736
Jigg

John Sheeles
(*fl.* 18th century)

1760
Minuet

Leopold Mozart
(1719–87)

The first roller-skates were designed by the Belgian Jean-Joseph Merlin. They turned out to be a disaster when demonstrated, and the four-wheeled versions in use today weren't patented until over a hundred years later, in 1863. The famous Royal Botanical Gardens were opened at Kew in London.

Leopold Mozart was the father of the famous Wolfgang Amadeus Mozart. As well as composing, Leopold was a violinist and wrote an important textbook on the art of violin playing.

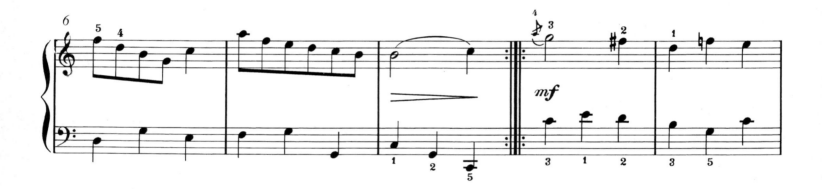

Tea from China became the British national drink around this time, and William Young of Philadelphia made shoes in pairs designed specifically for the left and right feet. In Rome, Count Alessandro Volta (after whom the 'volt' is named) invented the electric battery.

By the time of his death, Beethoven had become such a public figure that 10,000 people are said to have attended his funeral in Vienna. Though best known for his large-scale works, he wrote many smaller and easier pieces like this peasant dance.

1800
Allemande

Ludwig Van Beethoven
(1770–1827)

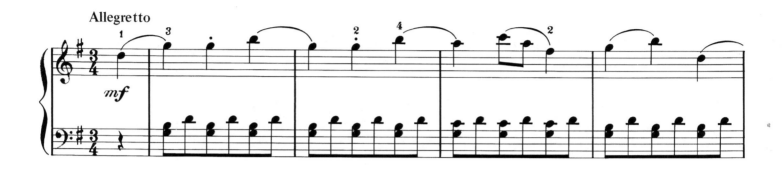

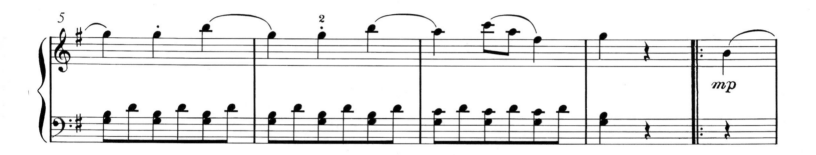

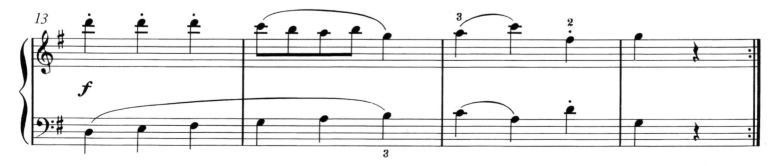

1815
Écossaise

Franz Schubert
(1797–1828)

Napoleon was finally defeated by the Duke of Wellington at the Battle of Waterloo and banished to the island of St Helena in the South Atlantic. Humphrey Davy developed the safety lamp for use in coal mines, with the result that canaries were no longer used to detect dangerous gases.

Schubert excelled at writing songs for voice and piano. They were often grouped together in 'song-cycles', such as *Winterreise* ('A Winter's Journey'). He also wrote a number of short dances; *Écossaise* is the French for 'Scottish Dance'.

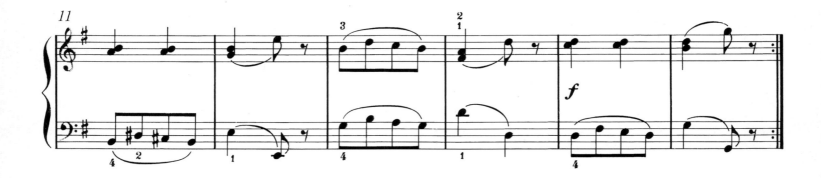

The paddle-steamer *Savannah* was the first steamship to cross the Atlantic. Her arrival off the coast of Ireland, with smoke bellowing from her funnel, made people on the shore think she was on fire and about to sink.

Weber is perhaps best known for his great operas. He also wrote some attractive piano music, and this piece represents a ballroom scene.

1819

Invitation to the Dance

Carl Maria von Weber
(1786–1826)

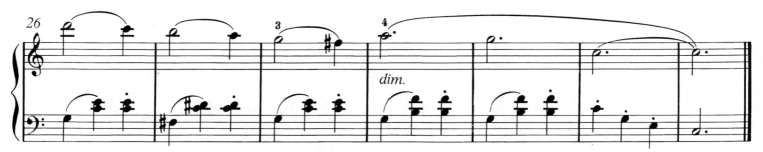

1839
Prelude

Fryderyk Chopin
(1810–49)

An American officer, Abner Doubleday, is reputed to have organized the first baseball game. William Henry Fox Talbot invented a process for making any number of prints from one negative, allowing the mass production of black-and-white photographs. He did it, he said, because he couldn't draw!

Although Chopin had a legendary reputation as a pianist, he disliked public performances. Most of his appearances were in fashionable society drawing-rooms, where his Romantic style was in great demand.

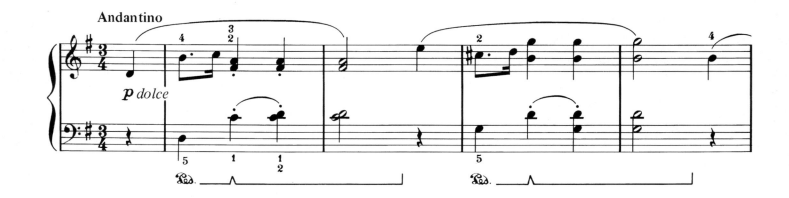

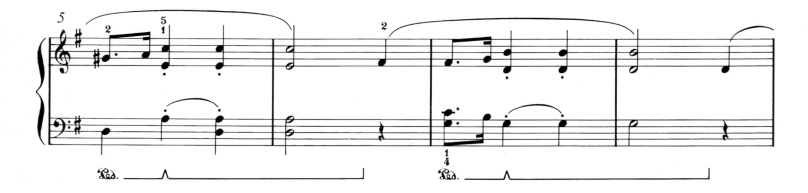

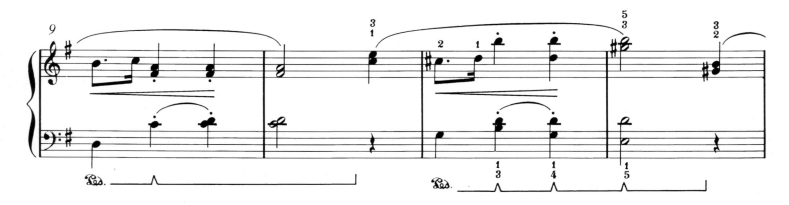

Morse code, named after its inventor, Samuel Morse, was used for the first time.
It represents the alphabet by a series of electronic beeps, long and short, which
can be passed down a telegraph wire for long-distance communication.
Alexander Dumas wrote *The Three Musketeers*.

Hungarian-born Stephen Heller published 160 piano pieces. After a concert tour
at the age of fourteen, he suffered a nervous breakdown, but eventually settled
in Paris, where he made a living as a critic and a composer of piano music.

L' Avalanche

Stephen Heller
(1813–88)

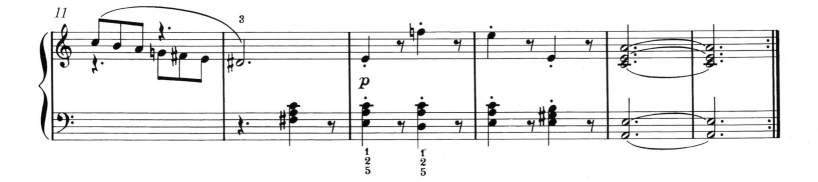

1846
Fandango

Christian Köhler
(1820–86)

Potato famine in Ireland killed many thousands of people and led to mass emigration to the USA. The first cheap newspaper was printed in England—the Daily News, editor Charles Dickens. The first surgical operation using anaesthetic took place in the USA.

Christian Köhler, a German piano teacher, is remembered chiefly for his educational piano pieces. He also wrote large-scale works including an opera and a ballet.

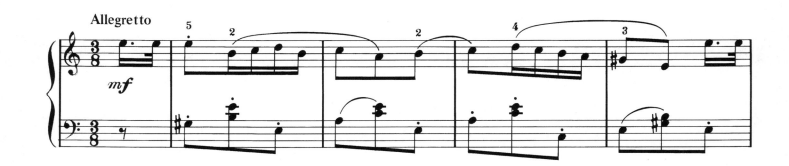

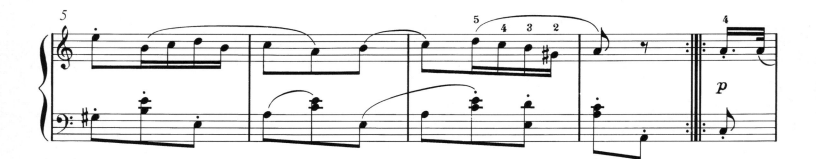

In France, social unrest developed into a full-scale revolution as the downtrodden masses turned their anger on those in power. The Communist Manifesto, a book outlining Communist beliefs, was written in London by Karl Marx and Friedrich Engels.

This piece comes from Schumann's *Album for the Young*—a collection of short character pieces, each painting a picture in music.

1848
Wild Horsemen

Robert Schumann
(1810–56)

17

Mikhail Glinka
(1804–57)

The speed of light was first measured by the French physicist Armand Fizeau—it is 186,000 miles per second, and at that rate it takes about $8\frac{1}{4}$ minutes for light to reach earth from the sun.

Glinka was a Russian composer who was fascinated by folk-dance rhythms and often borrowed them in his compositions. The polka is a dance which originated in Bohemia, later becoming one of the most popular nineteenth-century ballroom dances.

Sparrows were imported to the USA from Germany as a defence against caterpillars! London's Paddington station was designed by Brunel and Wyatt, and the Frenchman Henri Guifford made the first airship flight.

A tarantella is a Neapolitan dance which probably takes its name from Taranto, a town in the heel of Italy's famous 'boot' shape, or perhaps from a poisonous spider found there—the tarantula!

1852
Tarantella

Johann Friedrich Burgmüller
(1806–74)

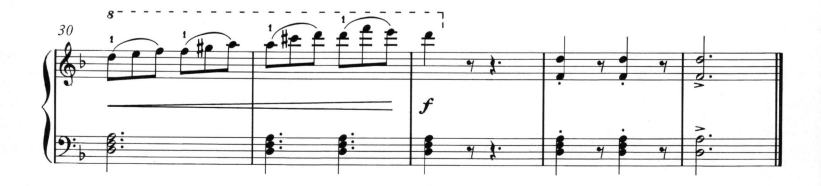

The year of the mysterious 'Marie Celeste' case—a ship found deserted in mid-Atlantic, the crew gone, food on the tables, and 1,700 barrels of alcohol untouched. The mystery has never been solved. The first international soccer match was played between England and Scotland—it ended in a goalless draw.

Bizet wrote this march as incidental music for a play called *The Maid of Arles*. The music is based on a Provençal Christmas carol often known as the 'March of the Three Kings'.

March from 'L' Arlésienne'

Georges Bizet
(1838–75)

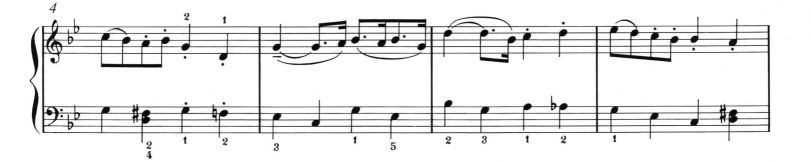

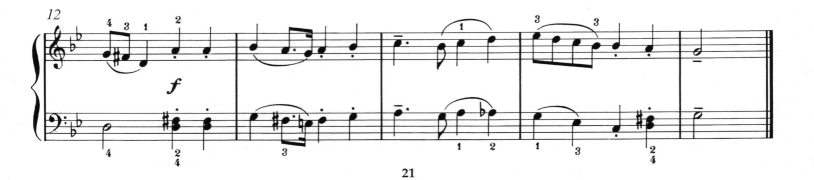

1875
Waltz

Fritz Spindler
(1817–1905)

The Chimney Sweep Act was passed, making it illegal to send 'climbing boys', who were often appallingly treated, up chimneys to clean them. 'General' William Booth founded the Salvation Army.

The German pianist, teacher, and composer Fritz Spindler was a great animal lover. It is said that he kept enough animals in his garden to fill a small zoo!

Allegretto con grazia

Thomas Edison invented the phonograph, the forerunner of today's cassette and CD players, recording the historic words 'Mary had a little lamb'. The first Wimbledon Tennis Championship was held.

Theodor Kullak was just one of a whole family of German musicians. He was a pupil of the great Austrian pianist Karl Czerny, and founded his own music school in Berlin. A berceuse is a lullaby and often features a gentle rocking rhythm.

Berceuse

Theodor Kullak
(1818–82)

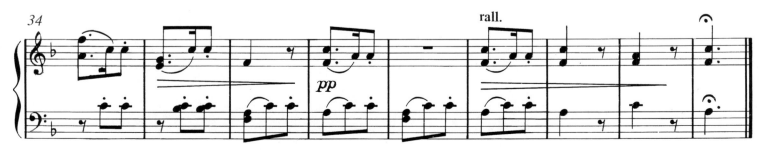

1899
Maple Leaf Rag

Scott Joplin
(1868–1917)

Aspirin was marketed for the first time. Sigmund Freud published his *Interpretation of Dreams*, changing the way we think about our dreams and the unconscious mind. The first magnetic sound recording was made.

Scott Joplin's music was largely forgotten for many years, but became very popular again in the 1970s after being used in the film *The Sting*.

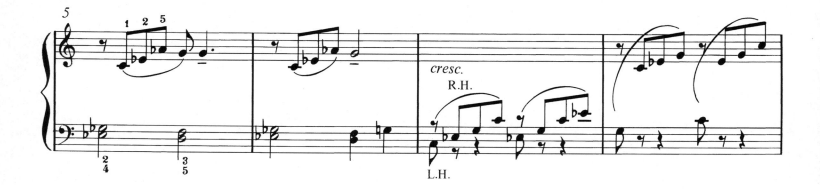

Fine

D.C. al Fine

25

1903
Christmas Present

Vladimir Rebikov
(1866–1920)

The Wright brothers achieved the first powered flight in North Carolina, USA—it lasted fifty-nine seconds. The first teddy bear was produced, named after the US President, Theodore 'Teddy' Roosevelt. In Britain, a speed limit of twenty miles per hour was introduced on the roads.

Rebikov was a Russian composer. His early works show the influence of Tchaikovsky, but his style developed and he became interested in modern ideas such as combining music and mime in a piano piece.

The Frenchman Louis Blériot made the first powered flight across the English Channel, just six years after the first powered flight ever. He won £1000, and the journey took 43 minutes from Calais to Dover.

Samuil Maikapar was a professor at the St Petersburg Conservatory in Russia for over 20 years. He wrote a great many pieces for piano.

Samuil Maikapar
(1867–1916)

Allegro giocoso

1960
Pagoda

Soulima Stravinsky
(1910–)

John F. Kennedy became President of the USA, only to be tragically assassinated three years later in Dallas, Texas. The film director Alfred Hitchcock (who always made a short appearance in his films) made his famous thriller *Psycho*.

Soulima Stravinsky is the son of the great Igor Stravinsky. He is a pianist, and has written a number of large-scale works as well as shorter, easier pieces for young players.

This piece uses black keys only.

In Iran, the Islamic fundamentalist leader the Ayatollah Khomeini replaced the Shah. The USSR occupied Afghanistan, and Margaret Thatcher became the first female Prime Minister of Great Britain.

Hugh Seal is a clergyman. He studied with W. H. 'Billy' Reed—leader of the London Symphony Orchestra during the period that Elgar was at his most creative, and a close friend of the great composer.

Hugh Seal
(1910–)

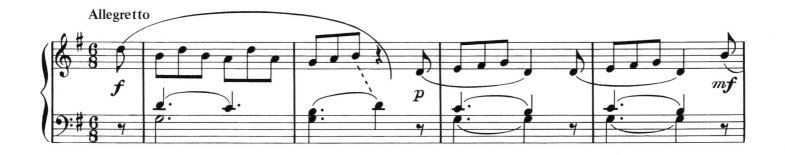

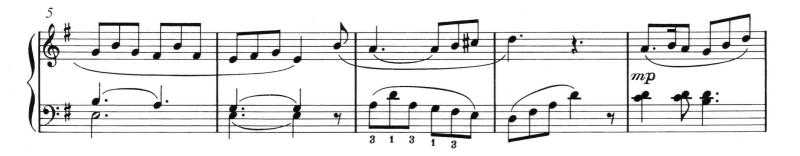

Reproduced by permission of the composer.

1990
Oriental March

Paul Harris
(1957–)

This march evokes the atmopshere of distant lands.
Be sure to look closely at the dynamics and make the
contrast between staccato and legato playing.

Allegro marziale

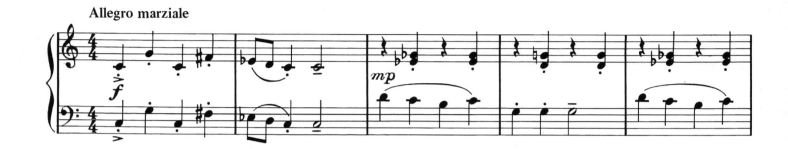

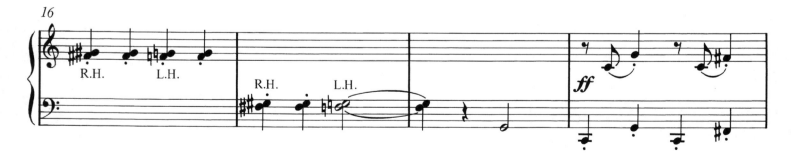

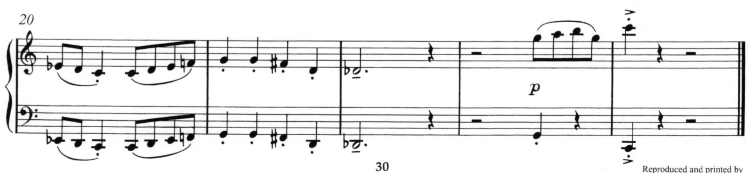

Reproduced and printed by
Halstan & Co. Ltd., Amersham, Bucks., England